BUILDING WORKS

THEATER

John Malam

CONTENTS

The fold-out section at the start of this book shows the theater building from the outside. Open it up to reveal a cutaway view of the inside, with a key to what happens in each area. After this, you will find a plan of the auditorium and stage.

PETER BEDRICK BOOKS
NTC/Contemporary Publishing Group

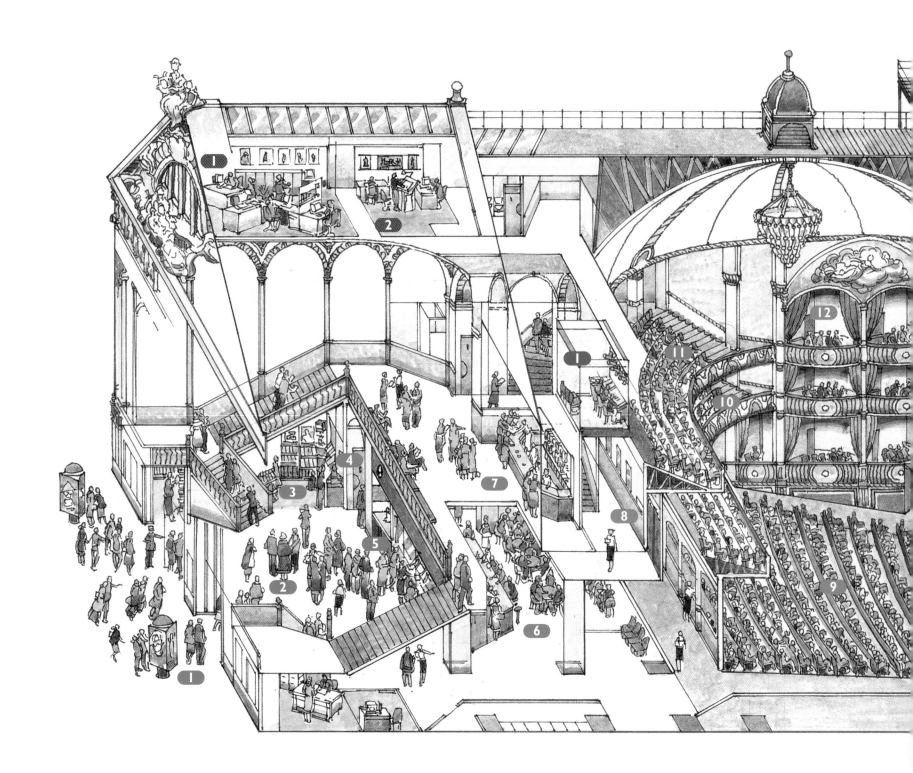

Inside a theater

The theater described in this book is a traditional proscenium theater. It can be divided into three main areas, which are color-coded and numbered in this cutaway picture. To find out what happens in each area, use the key on either side of the main picture. The three areas are:

1 Front of house
These are all the areas of the theater, shown in green, to which the audience has access.

2 The stage
This refers to the acting area and all the parts of the building above and around it—they are shown in blue.

3 Backstage
These are the areas which the audience does not see, and does not have access to. They are shown in red.

The symbol at the top of some pages is a simplified plan of the front of house and stage, showing which part of the theater you are reading about. If you are backstage, different symbols indicate what goes on there. For example, an explosion symbol means that you are in the special effects workshop. On each right-hand page you will find a list of the room numbers that correspond to the cutaway picture.

Some of the more unusual words used in this book are explained in the glossary on page 30.

Front of house

1 Main entrance
The front of the theater is decorated with posters advertising the show.

2 Foyer
The audience gathers here before the start of a show, and during the intermission.

3 Bookshop
The shop sells books about acting and theater, as well as souvenirs such as T-shirts, key rings and posters.

4 Restrooms

5 Box office
People buy programs and tickets here. The box office also takes reservations by phone.

6 Restaurant and café

7 Bar
This area is usually busiest during the intermission, when the audience leaves the auditorium for refreshments.

8 Auditorium entrance
The auditorium is the part of the theater where the audience sits.

9 Stalls
Most of the audience sits in these seats, on the ground floor of the auditorium.

10 Dress circle
This is the middle level of seats in the auditorium.

11 Gallery
This is the highest level of seats in the auditorium, and is sometimes known as the gods.

12 Boxes
These are small, private sections of the auditorium, with seats for just a few people.

13 Pit
When a performance requires music, the orchestra sits in this sunken area. At other times the pit is covered over with extra seats or a stage extension.

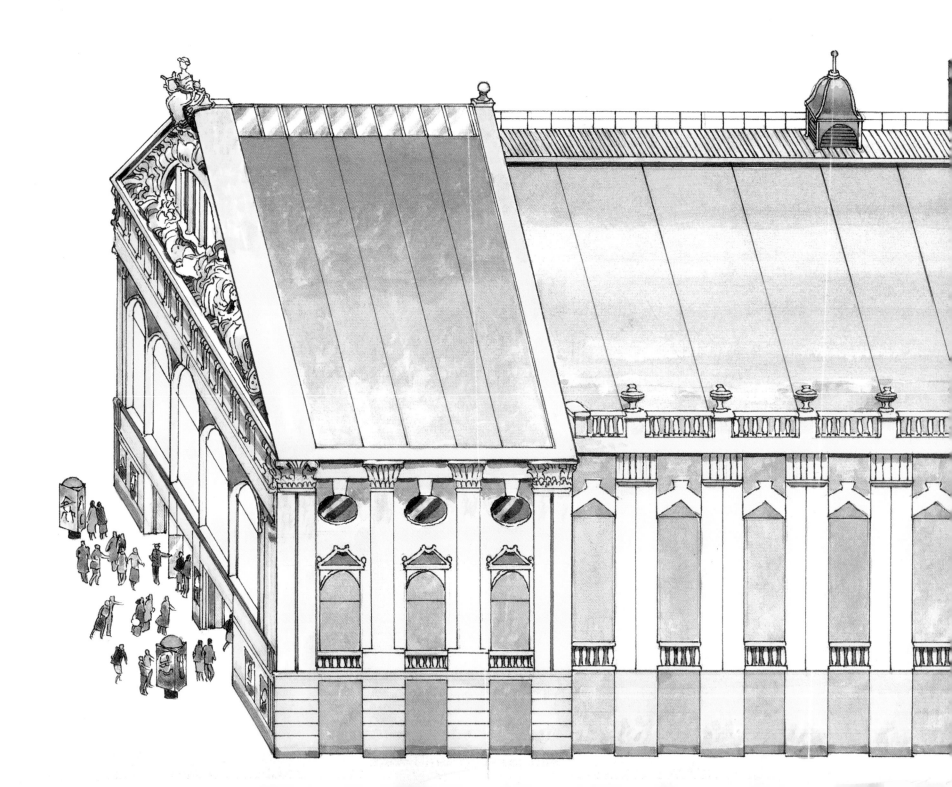

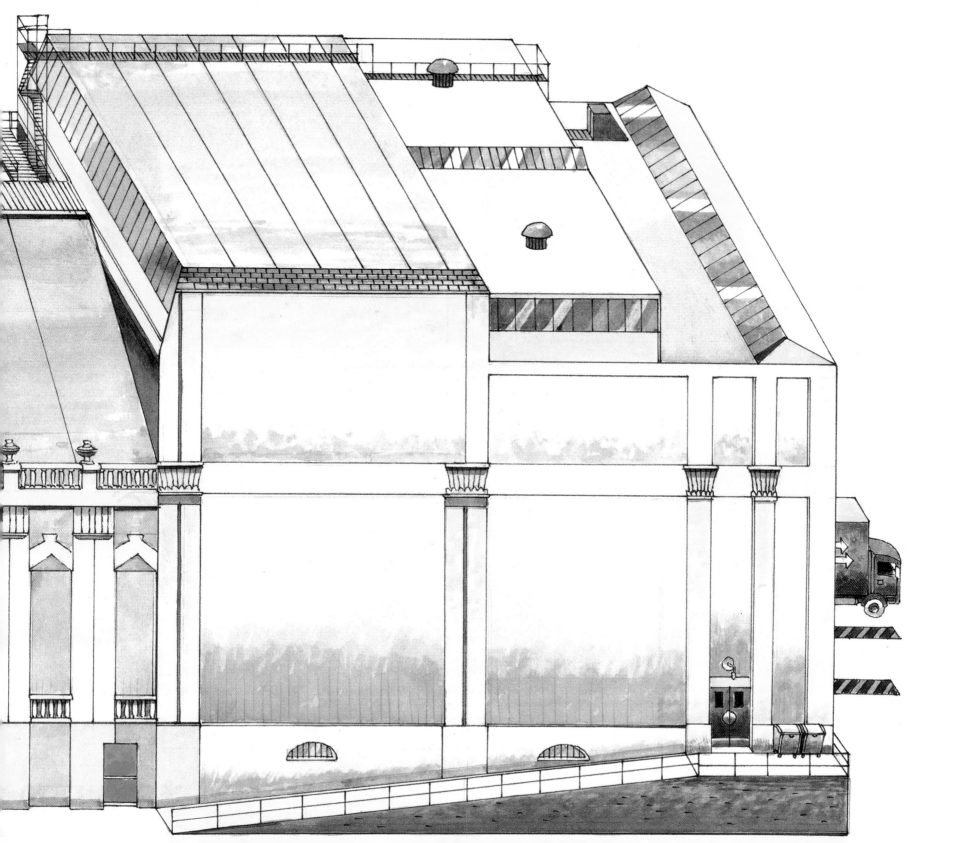

The stage

1 Light and sound rooms
During a performance, operators in these rooms control light and sound effects.

2 Apron
The narrow strip of stage which lies in front of the curtain.

3 Stage
This is where actors perform the show. In many theaters the stage slopes upwards from front to back.

4 Proscenium arch
This decorative arch frames the stage, and is the boundary between the audience and the acting area.

5 Safety curtain
This fireproof steel shutter can be lowered to protect the audience from a fire on the stage.

6 Lighting bars
Theater lights are attached to these metal bars. In some theaters the bars are reached by ladder or scaffolding. In others they can be lowered to the ground.

7 Flies or fly tower
During a performance, scenery backdrops are held high up in the flies, out of sight of the audience, ready to be lowered to the stage.

8 Fly gallery
The flying crew work on this platform above the stage, raising and lowering scenery backdrops.

9 Trap
This trap door opens to allow a performer to appear and disappear.

10 Prompt desk
The stage manager supervises a performance from this corner, and keeps in contact with the light and sound room.

11 Wings
Performers wait here, at the sides of the stage, before making their entrance. Sometimes small props are kept in the wings too.

12 Slip stage
This is a large platform on wheels that carries a complete scene. It is stored in the wings and pushed on to the stage when needed.

13 Scenery, props and special effects workshops
Here props and pieces of scenery are created by designers, carpenters and painters. Special effects are made here too.

 # Backstage

1 Management offices
In these rooms the theater manager ensures the smooth running of the building, and the theater director plans the program of events.

2 Publicity department
The publicity team puts together programs and sends out leaflets about upcoming events.

3 Rehearsal rooms
Performers read through the script and hold rehearsals here.

4 Wig room
Wigs are stored here, on head blocks kept on shelves.

5 Cast dressing rooms
These rooms are shared by the members of the cast (the less well known actors). Here they change into their costumes and put on make-up and wigs.

6 Restrooms

7 Wardrobe department
Actors' costumes are made, cleaned, repaired and stored in this large room.

8 Stars' dressing rooms
The leading actors have their own private dressing rooms.

9 Delivery bay
Very large props and pieces of scenery are delivered here, at the back of the theater.

10 Stage door
Performers enter and leave the theater by this back door.

11 Scenery dock
Tall pieces of scenery are stored here, beside the stage.

12 Store rooms
Old scenery and props are kept in these basement rooms.

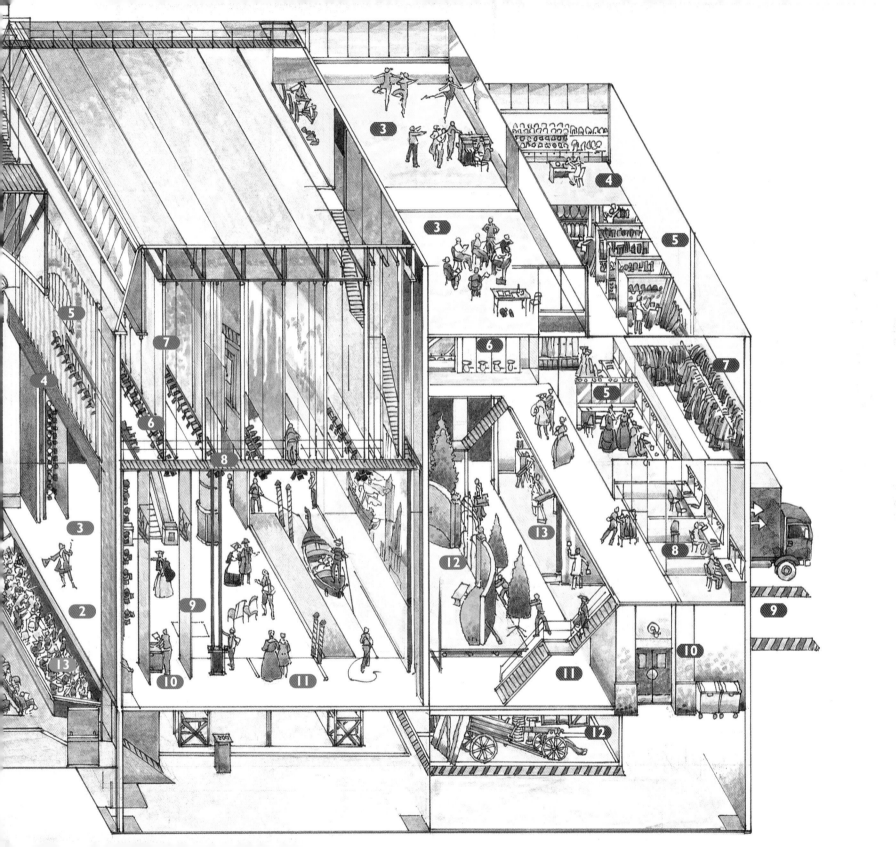

What is a theater?

The word theater comes from an old Greek word meaning "a place for seeing." Today, just as in ancient Greece, a theater is a place where different types of entertainment are performed in front of an audience. Plays, ballets, and operas are three of the most popular types of performance.

No two theaters are exactly the same. In a traditional proscenium theater the audience sits in a single block facing the stage. In a theater-in-the-round the audience surrounds a circular stage.

Preparing for a performance can take weeks or months. The actors, or cast, rehearse their roles with the director; designers devise sets (the scenery) and carpenters make them; costume makers prepare clothes, shoes, wigs and jewelry; the lighting is designed and tried out; special effects are set up and tested; musicians practice the musical score; and publicists prepare posters and programs.

By the time of the opening night, every member of the production team and the cast knows exactly what they are supposed to do, and at what point in the show they must do it. Timing is all-important for the show to be a success.

As the lights in the auditorium go down, the show begins. The cast performs on stage, while the other members of the team carry out their vital jobs behind the scenes, out of sight of the audience.

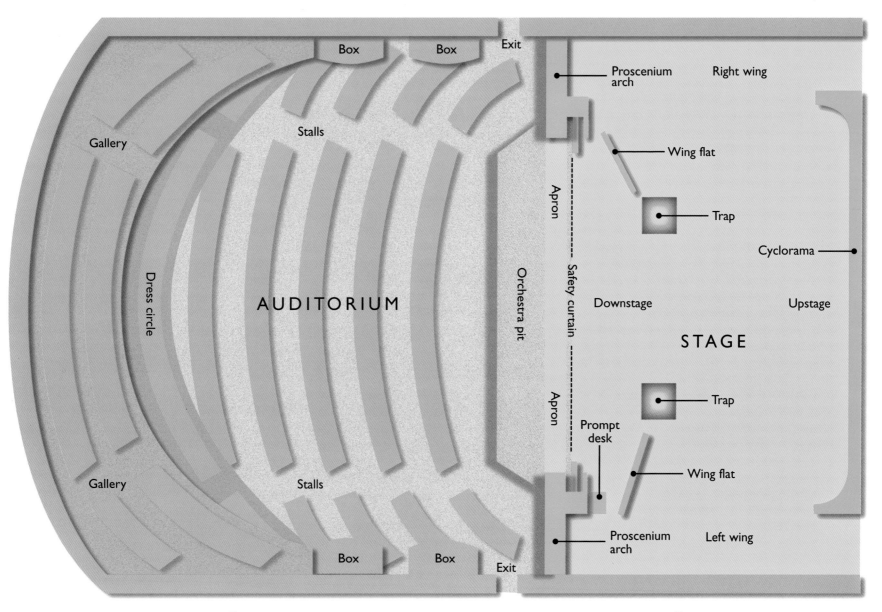

Box

Box

Exit

Gallery

Stalls

Proscenium arch

Right wing

Wing flat

Trap

Cyclorama

Apron

Dress circle

Orchestra pit

Safety curtain

Downstage

Upstage

AUDITORIUM

STAGE

Trap

Prompt desk

Gallery

Stalls

Wing flat

Box

Box

Exit

Proscenium arch

Left wing

⬤ In a proscenium theater, the audience sits in a block facing the stage. The seats on the ground floor are called the stalls. Above the stalls is a higher level of seats called the dress circle. The highest seats are in the gallery.

⬤ The stage in a proscenium theater is rectangular. On each side of the stage are the wings, where actors wait before going on stage. The wings cannot be seen by the audience.

Foyer and box office

The main entrance to the theater is lit up brightly before an evening performance. Posters and banners advertise the show and its leading actors. An attendant in uniform greets people as they arrive.

In the theater foyer people buy tickets and programs. A bookshop sells books about theaters, actors and playwrights. Scripts are on sale, mainly to students and people who want to perform the plays themselves. Key rings, T-shirts and posters are popular too.

The ticket kiosk in a theater is called the box office. The name dates back several hundred years to when most theater seats were in small boxes, rather than rows as they are today. A successful show—one that makes a profit from ticket sales—is described as a box office hit. An unsuccessful show is a box office flop.

▼ The Muses were nine Greek goddesses of the arts. Traditional theater foyers are often decorated with statues of Melpomene (representing tragedy), Terpsichore (dance) and Thalia (comedy).

Muse statue

Stairs to dress circle

Bookshop

Attendant

2

Cloakroom

Box office

Stairs to dress circle

Canopy

◭ Cabinets at the front of the theater display posters, newspaper reviews and photographs of the show.

The foyer bar serves drinks before the start of a show and during the intermission. The theater café is also open during the evening, selling snacks and light meals. The foyer also has a coat check area, where the theater will hold peoples' coats during the performance for a small fee.

People do not wait long in the foyer. As soon as they have bought tickets and programs they make their way to their seats in the auditorium.

The auditorium

The word auditorium comes from the Latin word *auditorius*—a place for hearing. This is the part of the theater where the audience watches and listens to the show. The seats are arranged in rows. Aisles along the sides divide the rows into blocks.

The seats on the ground floor are called stalls. Many people think these are the best seats in the theater. Above them is the dress circle—an old name from the days when the audience was expected to wear formal evening dress.

Some old theaters have an even higher level of seats, called the gallery or the gods. These are the cheapest seats in the theater. The people who sit high up in the gallery have always tended to be the noisiest members of the audience!

▶ The set designer uses a sightline diagram like this one to make sure the lights around the stage and any scenery in the flies are hidden from the audience.

Scenery stored in the flies

Gallery

Stalls

4

Box

Dress circle

Box

Stalls

◀ Ushers check tickets and show members of the audience to their seats. People who arrive after the start of a show may not be allowed to take their seats until the intermission or a scene change.

The floors of the stalls, dress circle and gallery slope gently down to the stage. This gives everyone a good view of the action.

The small, private balconies at the sides of the auditorium are called boxes. Each box has seats for just a few people. They are often used by famous people who do not want to be seen by the audience. A few theaters in Britain have a royal box. This can only be used by members of the royal family, or by important visitors from abroad.

The designer of the show's stage set—its scenery and props—has to be certain that the audience can see as much of the set as possible. But some things must be kept out of sight. These are hidden in the wings, or in the flies above the stage, until they need to be brought into view.

As the audience enters the auditorium, ushers check tickets and show people to their seats.

The pit

Between the stage and the front seats in the stalls is a large area sunk into the ground. This is the pit, where the orchestra performs the music for a show.

In some theaters the pit extends under the front part of the stage. The musicians sit below ground level, and cannot be seen by the audience. They usually dress in formal clothes—men in black dinner jackets and bow ties, and women in long dresses.

For a show without music, the pit can be covered over. Some theaters have lifts which raise the floor of the pit up to the level of the stalls. Extra seats can be placed over the concealed pit, or the acting area can be extended into the auditorium by adding a removable stage called a forestage.

▶ Some orchestra pits extend far below the stage. The musicians are hidden from the audience, who have a clear view of the stage.

Wind section

String section

Brass
section

Percussion
section

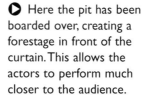
Here the pit has been boarded over, creating a forestage in front of the curtain. This allows the actors to perform much closer to the audience.

Conductor

String
section

7

An opera or a ballet requires a full-size orchestra. There is a string section (violins, double basses and cellos), a wind section (flutes, oboes, clarinets, piccolos and bassoons), a brass section (horns, trumpets, trombones and tubas) and a percussion section (drums, cymbals and triangles). There may be harps, pianos and organs too. Fewer instruments are used in shows that mix speaking and singing parts, such as a musical.

The conductor stands on a raised box called a podium, facing towards the musicians and away from the audience. The conductor holds a short wand, called a baton, which is waved in the air to beat time to the music. The musicians follow the signals to play faster or slower.

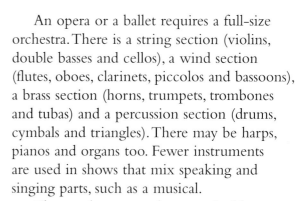

The stage

The stage is the acting area of the theater, raised up from ground level in front of the stalls. The space it takes up inside the theater is known as the stagehouse.

Theaters often have a raked stage, which slopes upwards from front to back. This has given us the terms upstage (towards the back of the stage) and downstage (towards the front).

The part of the stage nearest the audience is the apron, which lies in front of the curtain. Sometimes actors use this narrow strip of stage while scenery is changed behind the curtain.

Behind the apron is the proscenium arch, which frames the action on stage. The word proscenium comes from a Greek word meaning "before the stage." The arch divides the audience from the stage and is the boundary between the front of the house and the backstage area. It also holds up the ceiling of the theater.

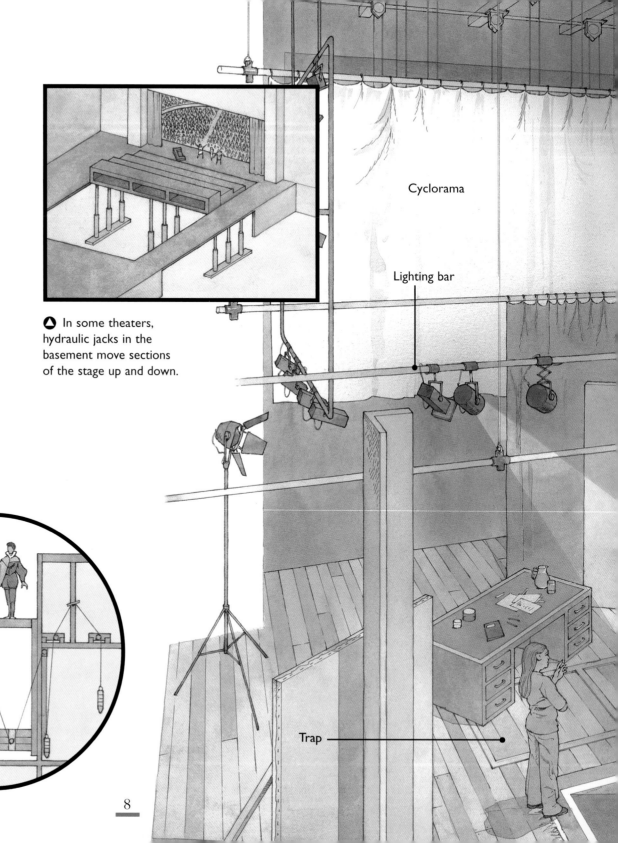

▲ In some theaters, hydraulic jacks in the basement move sections of the stage up and down.

▶ A cross-section through a stage trap. Weights are used to raise and lower an actor to and from the stage.

Cyclorama

Lighting bar

Trap

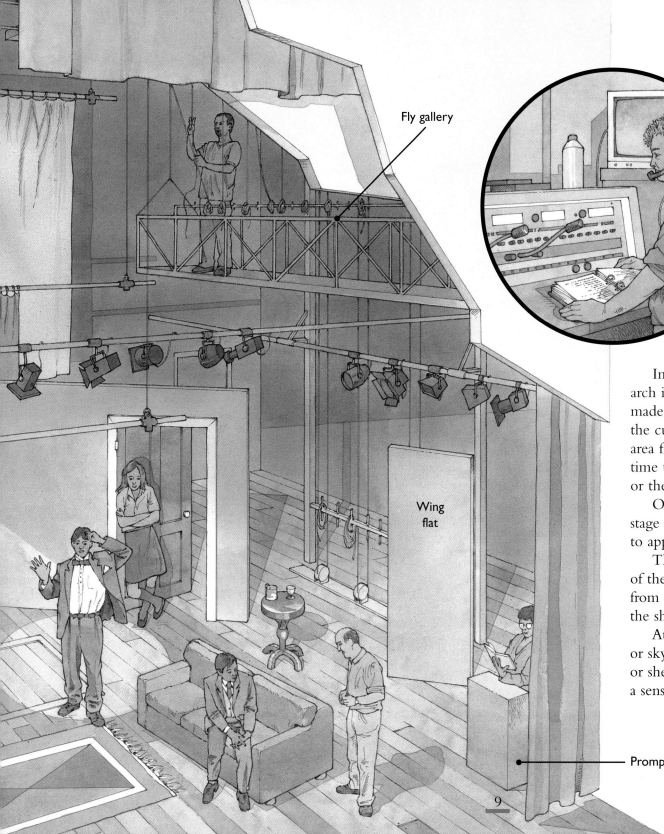

Fly gallery

During a show, the stage manager talks to the stagehands through a microphone attached to a headset. The headset has only one earpiece, so the manager can listen to the performance at the same time.

Immediately behind the proscenium arch is the safety curtain—a fireproof shutter made from steel. If a fire breaks out on stage, the curtain is lowered to seal off the acting area from the auditorium, giving the audience time to escape. It is also called the iron curtain or the fire curtain.

On the stage floor are trap doors, called stage traps, which open to allow a performer to appear and disappear.

The prompt desk is tucked inside one of the wings at the side of the stage, hidden from the audience. The stage manager runs the show from here.

At the back of the stage is the cyclorama, or skycloth. This is an undecorated backcloth, or sheet, usually curved at each end. It gives a sense of space and height to the stage.

Wing flat

Prompt desk

9

Wings and flies

The wings are on either side of the stage, out of sight of the audience. Actors wait in the wings until they make their entrance on stage. If a performer arrives too early or too late, this is known as bad timing.

During a performance the wings are always busy. If there is enough space, props and small pieces of furniture are laid out here, ready to be taken on stage. The wings must be kept as uncluttered as possible, to allow actors to come and go freely.

Large flat panels covered with painted canvas, called wing flats, extend the area of the wings on to the edge of the stage. They face the audience, usually at a slight angle. They make the stage area smaller. Actors stand behind them, ready to make their entrance.

High above the stage, out of sight of the audience, is the fly tower, or flies. Pieces of scenery, especially backdrops, are stored here during a performance. A backdrop is also known as a backcloth. It is a large sheet, painted with a scene, that hangs at the back of the stage.

▶ If a theater does not have a tall fly tower to store backdrops, they are wrapped around rollers.

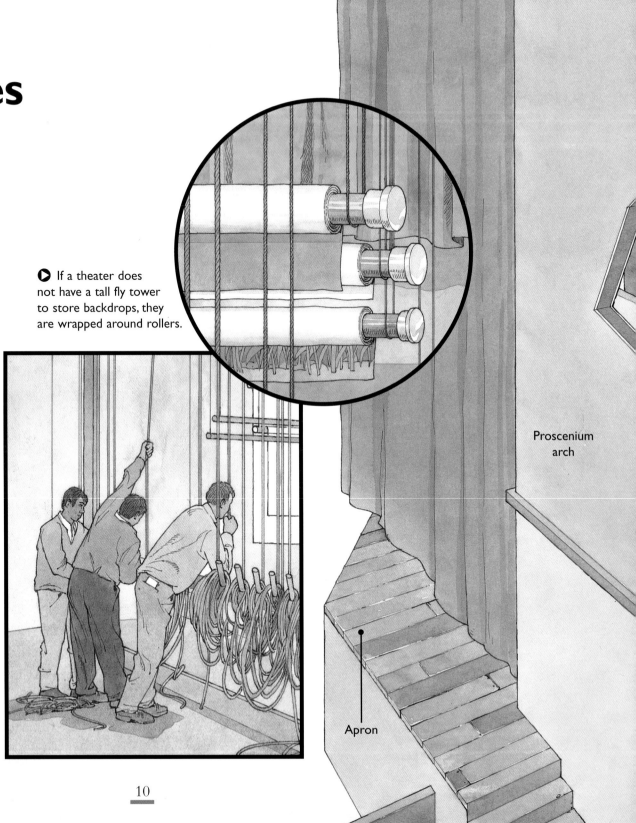

Proscenium arch

Apron

▶ Backdrops are usually lowered down to the stage by hand. If a member of the fly crew shouts "Heads below!" the people on stage take cover. It means that something has been dropped from the fly gallery.

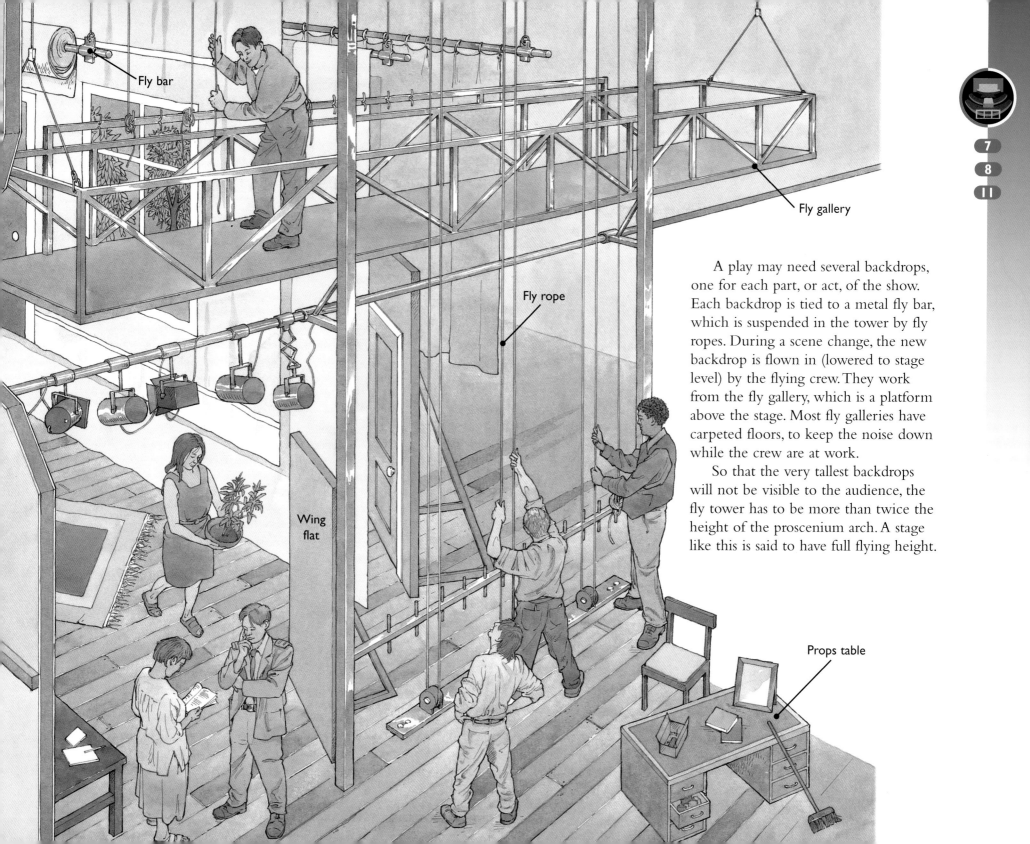

Fly bar

Fly gallery

Fly rope

Wing
flat

Props table

A play may need several backdrops,
one for each part, or act, of the show.
Each backdrop is tied to a metal fly bar,
which is suspended in the tower by fly
ropes. During a scene change, the new
backdrop is flown in (lowered to stage
level) by the flying crew. They work
from the fly gallery, which is a platform
above the stage. Most fly galleries have
carpeted floors, to keep the noise down
while the crew are at work.

So that the very tallest backdrops
will not be visible to the audience, the
fly tower has to be more than twice the
height of the proscenium arch. A stage
like this is said to have full flying height.

Light and sound

The lighting and sound control rooms are at the back of the auditorium. Light and sound operators work at computerized consoles. These are wired up to lamps and loudspeakers on stage and in the auditorium.

Theater lighting has three functions—to make the actors visible to the audience, to create the mood for the show, and to highlight the costumes and the stage set. Lighting operators need to have a good view of the auditorium and the stage, allowing them to check that the lights are working correctly.

Theater lamps, or lanterns, are suspended above the stage on metal lighting bars. The bars are reached by ladders or scaffold towers, or they are flown in (lowered down) to the stage. The lanterns are clamped tightly to the bars by a team of lighting assistants.

There are hundreds of different types of lamps. They are not only used for shining light—some project pictures on to the stage to create special effects such as clouds, snow, fire, smoke or rain.

◗ There are three main types of theater lamps.

1 A floodlight shines a wash of light across a wide area.

2 A spotlight shines a small circle of light. The size of the circle can be changed.

3 A beamlight shines a strong, straight line of light. The width of the beam is fixed.

Lighting bar

Lighting assistant

Lighting bar flown in to stage

Lighting console

Sound mixing desk

◀ The sound of the wind is produced by a wooden drum spinning against a piece of canvas.

During a show, microphones around the stage pick up the actors' voices and music from the orchestra. Sometimes actors wear tiny microphones, hidden in their costumes or wigs.

The sounds are transmitted to a console in the control room. The sound operator adjusts their loudness and sends them to the correct loudspeakers in the auditorium.

Sound effects, such as wind, rain and thunder, can be created live during a show or pre-recorded on to tape or CD. During the performance, the sound operator follows a cue sheet, which lists exactly when every sound effect must be played.

▼ A simple outline shape is projected on to the stage by a thin metal sheet called a gobo. The gobo is fitted into the slot on the front of a lamp.

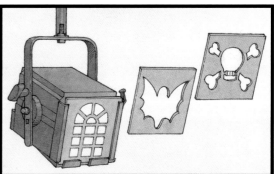

Scenery and props

Behind the stage is the scenery workshop. Here designers, carpenters and painters make most of the scenery for the shows staged at the theater.

Scenery tells the audience where the action in the show takes place. A show might have several acts, each one needing a change of scenery.

The scenery designer starts by making a scale model of the stage. Tiny versions of the scenery are added to the model. When everyone is happy with the design, the carpenters begin work on the full-size scenery.

The most basic piece of scenery is called a flat. This is a wooden frame with painted canvas stretched over it. On the stage, flats are joined together to make three-dimensional pieces of scenery.

Scenery is designed so that it can be put up and taken down quickly. Pieces can be suspended above the stage in the flies, ready to be lowered down between acts. Some scenery is fixed to a movable platform called a slip stage. It is kept in the wings, ready to be wheeled on stage.

There are three categories of props: hand props (left), such as swords and books; dressings (center), such as paintings and plants; and furnishings (right), including thrones and desks.

Very large pieces of scenery are delivered to the loading bay.

Flat

Wooden frame for flat

Flat

While scenery is being built, the properties workshop makes, buys or borrows all the small items, called props, for the show. A good prop has to look like the real article. Attention to detail is important, especially for historical props. Designers visit museums, libraries and stately homes to find out what old objects were like.

Prop designers use many tricks to convince an audience they are looking at a real object. For example, joints of meat are made from papier mâché. Cabbages and cauliflowers are made from coloured cloth. Fresh loaves of bread are painted with a special varnish called shellac. This stops them from rotting.

When the scenery and props are all together on stage, the whole display is called the set.

▼ The scenery designer uses a model made of balsa wood and card to try out different set designs.

15

Special effects

Next to the props workshop is a room where special effects are produced. A special effect is something that makes an impression on the audience. The impression can be almost anything, such as a sudden change of scenery, an explosion, a flashing light or a fire.

Transformation effects change the appearance of the set or the performers while the audience is watching. The change happens so quickly that the audience is left wondering how it has been done. For example, an actor or a piece of scenery can be made to appear and disappear by using a finely woven cloth called a gauze.

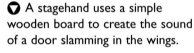

○ A snow bag contains tiny pieces of polystyrene or paper. The pieces flutter to the stage like snowflakes when the bag is shaken.

△ An actor bursts through a star trap on to the stage.

▽ A stagehand uses a simple wooden board to create the sound of a door slamming in the wings.

The opening of a star trap is cut into hinged triangular pieces. As soon as an actor bursts through the star, the pieces snap shut. The performer seems to have risen through a solid floor!

Some effects are created very simply. Falling snow is produced by a snow bag which hangs above the stage in the flies. The sound of a door slamming is made by a simple wooden board. A stagehand pulls up one end of the board, and then lets it slam against the floor of the wings.

◁ When light shines from behind a gauze, an actor is visible to the audience. When light shines from the front, the gauze looks solid and the actor is invisible.

Some special effects use fireworks made specially for theaters. These are called pyrotechnics, or "pyros" for short. They make explosions, flashes and smoke effects, and are set off electrically from firing boxes.

Fake blood is made by mixing red and yellow food dye with a type of syrup called glycerine. Sometimes fake blood is contained in a capsule which an actor breaks with their teeth. The mixture is safe to swallow.

◗ A smoke machine works by heating a special liquid until it turns to gas. A fan blows the smoke across the stage.

◗ A scenery flat can be transformed with a roll of painted canvas. When the canvas drops down, the picture on the flat changes in the blink of an eye.

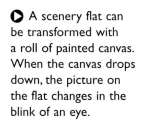

◖ A pyrotechnic on stage is connected to a firing box in the wings.

A popular effect used in comedies is the rat run. An object, such as a mouse or a string of sausages, appears to move across the stage by itself. In fact, it is pulled along a thin wire by a stagehand in the wings. The wire is fixed so that the object can climb up and down the scenery, and even fly over it.

You can read about the special effects created by the lighting and sound departments on pages 12-13.

Costumes and wigs

The costume, or wardrobe, department is where the actors' clothes are made, repaired, cleaned and ironed. Costume accessories, such as hats, shoes and jewelry, are also kept here.

The costume designer decides which clothes are needed for the show, how they should look, and which fabrics to make them from. The designer makes several sketches for each costume.

Actors are carefully measured for their costumes. Costume makers need to know a performer's height, the length of their arms and legs, as well as the size of their chest, waist, hips, feet and head. It helps to know whether the actor's ears are pierced too, just in case a character requires earrings.

The costume makers start to cut and sew the fabric, working from the designer's sketches and the actor's measurements. Some fabrics are dyed to produce the color the designer wants. Others need patterns stencilled on to them.

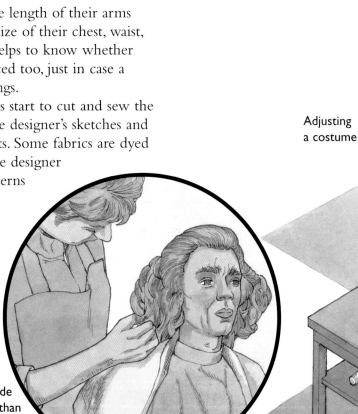

▶ A wig is specially made to fit an actor's head and hide their hair. It can take more than an hour to fit, or dress, a wig.

Wig

Head blocks

Washing machines

Adjusting a costume

Sewing machine

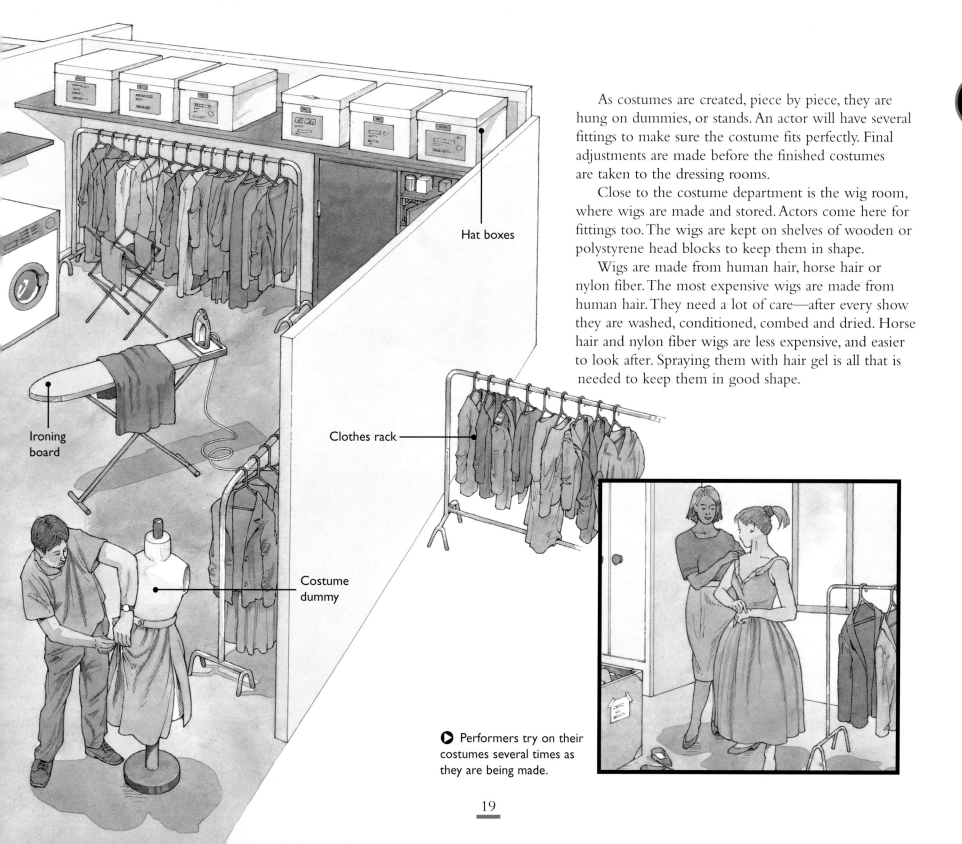

As costumes are created, piece by piece, they are hung on dummies, or stands. An actor will have several fittings to make sure the costume fits perfectly. Final adjustments are made before the finished costumes are taken to the dressing rooms.

Close to the costume department is the wig room, where wigs are made and stored. Actors come here for fittings too. The wigs are kept on shelves of wooden or polystyrene head blocks to keep them in shape.

Wigs are made from human hair, horse hair or nylon fiber. The most expensive wigs are made from human hair. They need a lot of care—after every show they are washed, conditioned, combed and dried. Horse hair and nylon fiber wigs are less expensive, and easier to look after. Spraying them with hair gel is all that is needed to keep them in good shape.

Hat boxes

Ironing board

Clothes rack

Costume dummy

▶ Performers try on their costumes several times as they are being made.

19

Dressing rooms and make-up

The dressing rooms are where actors put on make-up, change into costume, and get ready to go on stage. In some shows, actors have to change in and out of costumes very quickly. Because of this, dressing rooms are often close to the back of the stage.

There are two types of dressing rooms. The leading actors, or stars, each have their own room. The other actors, called the cast members, share dressing rooms. In large theaters the rooms are numbered, but because some actors are superstitious there is never a dressing room number 13.

In a dressing room, one entire wall is covered by mirrors and bright lights. Actors sit in front of the mirrors to have their make-up applied by make-up artists. Behind them are the costumes for the performance. The clothes hang on racks in the order they will be worn, to prevent an actor putting on the wrong costume by mistake.

◀ Traditional make-up, called greasepaint, is still used today. It can be messy and easily marks costumes. Modern make-up is cleaner and less greasy.

Mirror

Make-up artist

Clothes rack

20

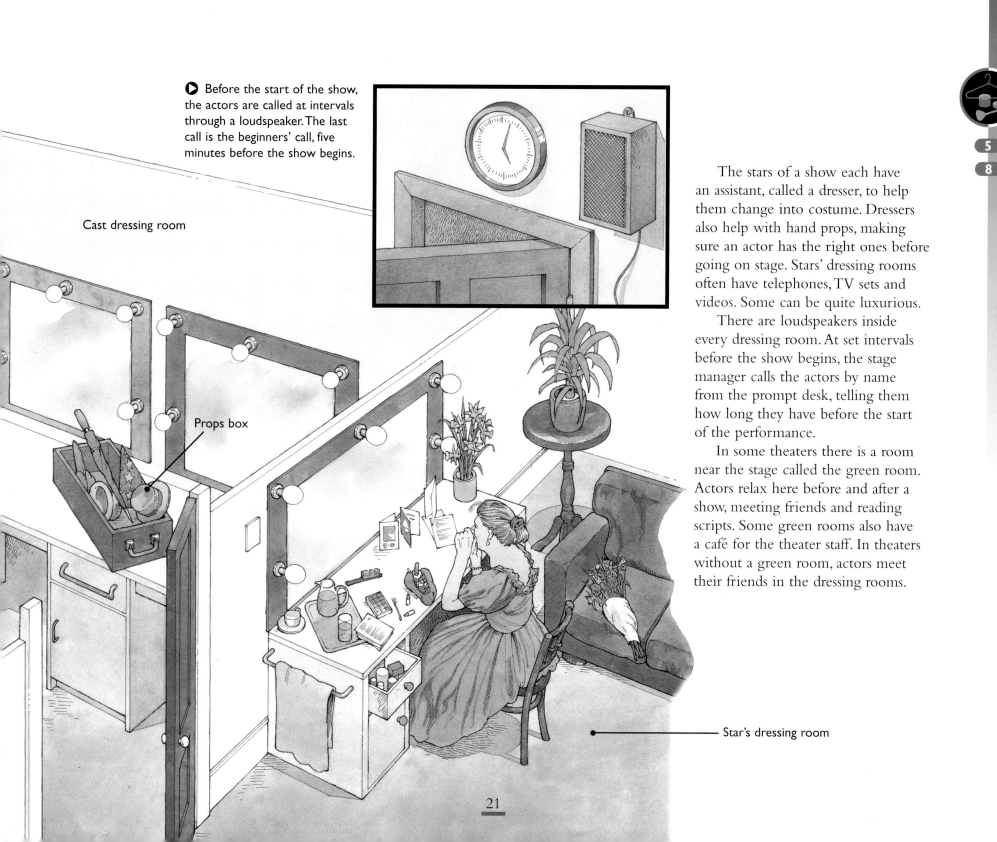

▶ Before the start of the show, the actors are called at intervals through a loudspeaker. The last call is the beginners' call, five minutes before the show begins.

Cast dressing room

Props box

Star's dressing room

The stars of a show each have an assistant, called a dresser, to help them change into costume. Dressers also help with hand props, making sure an actor has the right ones before going on stage. Stars' dressing rooms often have telephones, TV sets and videos. Some can be quite luxurious.

There are loudspeakers inside every dressing room. At set intervals before the show begins, the stage manager calls the actors by name from the prompt desk, telling them how long they have before the start of the performance.

In some theaters there is a room near the stage called the green room. Actors relax here before and after a show, meeting friends and reading scripts. Some green rooms also have a café for the theater staff. In theaters without a green room, actors meet their friends in the dressing rooms.

21

Rehearsal rooms

Rehearsal rooms are where actors practice the show before it is performed on stage. The director works with the cast to decide exactly how the show will be presented.

The first rehearsals are known as read-throughs, when actors read their parts from the script. They do not act or wear costumes. Read-throughs help actors to learn their lines and to know how their characters should be played.

Then the actors begin the actual rehearsals. At run-throughs, the whole play is performed, but the actors do not wear costumes. The floor of the rehearsal room is marked out with chalk or tape to show the positions of the scenery and props. Sometimes temporary scenery is used. This can be as simple as a wooden box.

During a technical rehearsal, light and sound engineers check the settings for their equipment. Stagehands practice moving the scenery and props, and the orchestra rehearses the music.

▷ At a script read-through the cast do not act or wear make-up.

Temporary prop

Director

22

Wooden posts to show position of doorway.

Colored tape to mark position of finished scenery.

Script

Temporary prop

○ A photographer taking pictures of a dress rehearsal. The photos are used for publicity—on posters and leaflets, and in the program.

During rehearsals the stage manager updates a master copy of the script. It shows when actors enter and exit the stage, and when light and sound effects are needed. The master script helps the stage manager to run a real performance smoothly from the prompt desk—and to prompt, or help out, actors who forget their lines.

Understudy rehearsals are held separately from the cast rehearsals. An understudy is an actor who learns a part being played by a leading actor. The understudy appears in the show in an emergency—if the leading actor becomes ill, for example.

Dress rehearsals are held in the days leading up to the opening night. The actors perform on stage in full costume, with real props and scenery. Publicity photographs are taken for the program and posters. The final rehearsal is sometimes performed in front of an invited audience, often groups of seniors or school children.

Types of theaters

All theaters can trace their origins back to the ancient Greeks, about 2500 years ago. Since then, theater buildings have evolved into many different types.

⬆ An ancient Greek theater, built into the side of a hill.

Ancient Greek theater

Greek theaters were built in the open air. The seats fitted into a natural hollow in the side of a hill. Plays were performed only in the daytime, by actors who spoke or sang their parts. They acted on a round patch of hard earth, and wore padded costumes and masks. A popular special effect was a crane which lifted an actor off the ground, making him appear to fly.

Proscenium theater

This is the type of theater described in this book. The stage is framed by an arch, called the proscenium. This divides the auditorium from the stage, separating the audience from the actors. The audience sits in a large block of seats facing the stage. Proscenium theaters first appeared in Europe in the 1600s. They are now the most common type of theater in the world.

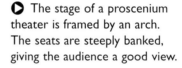

▶ The stage of a proscenium theater is framed by an arch. The seats are steeply banked, giving the audience a good view.

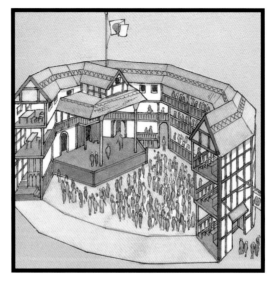

Playhouse theater

In the 1500s playhouses began to appear in major European cities. Before then, actors performed in the courtyards of inns and in the halls of large houses. Playhouses were usually circular and made of timber. Most of the audience stood up during the shows, which took place in daylight. Seats in the galleries were more expensive. The actors wore costumes, but little scenery and few props were used.

◀ A European playhouse theater from the 1500s.

Theater-in-the-round

Theaters-in-the-round first appeared in Europe in the Middle Ages, but went out of fashion with the arrival of the first proscenium theaters. The audience surrounds the stage on all sides, very close to the actors. This creates a very dramatic atmosphere. In the last 50 years theaters-in-the-round have become popular among more adventurous theater companies.

◀ Very little scenery can be used in theaters-in-the-round.

▲ Temporary outdoor theaters are sometimes built in the grounds of stately houses.

Outdoor theater

Most outdoor theaters are built in parks and other open spaces. Sometimes they are built in historic settings—within the walls of castles or in the grounds of stately homes. The stage is raised up from the ground, with seating set out in front or all around it. Performances can be held during the day or at night. All the materials used to build the theater have to be strong enough to withstand the weather, especially wind and rain.

Street theater

This type of theater became popular in the 1800s, when traveling players went from town to town with fold-away canvas booths and colorful puppets. The booths, which looked like miniature proscenium theaters, were set up in streets and on beaches. Modern street performers can be seen in many towns and cities. They often perform with no scenery and only a few props.

▶ One of the most popular street theater shows was *Punch and Judy*, which can still be seen today.

Theater history

The ancient Egyptians stage the first plays, at religious ceremonies.

c. 3200 BC

A Greek poet called Thespis wins the first ever dramatic competition.

534 BC

Athens is the theatrical capital of Greece. Two drama festivals are held every year, one for comedies, the other for tragedies.

500–300 BC

A 1200-seat theater is built at Epidauros, in Greece. It has a raised stage, wings and changing rooms.

340 BC

The first permanent Roman theater is built from stone. Before this date, Roman theaters were temporary wooden buildings.

55 BC

3200 BC to 1656

The first US theater is built at Williamsburg, in Virginia.

1716

The first theater programs, called playbills, are produced. They are glued to the walls of London theaters.

1737

Kado-za doll theater in Osaka, Japan, is the first theater to use a revolving stage.

1758

Orchestras begin to sit in a pit, below the level of the stage.

Late 1700s

Drury Lane Theatre in London is the first to use a fireproof safety curtain.

1800

1716 to present day

The world's first training school for actors is built in China.

800s AD

The age of mystery plays in Europe. These religious plays are performed in churches, market squares or on moving wagons.

1250–1500

The first public theaters are built in Spain (1520), France (1550), England (1576) and Italy (1584).

1500s

The Globe Theatre is built in London, England.

1599

At the Teatro Novissimo in Venice, Italy, weights are used to raise and lower backdrops.

1641

At the Theatre Royal, London, large tanks of water are used to stage sea battles.

1804

The California Theater in San Francisco, California, is the first US theater to use electric stage lamps.

1879

The Lyceum Theatre, London, begins to draw curtains across the stage, to show that a scene has ended.

1881

The world's biggest theater opens, in Beijing, China. It seats 10,000 spectators.

1959

A replica of the sixteenth-century Globe Theatre is opened in London.

1997

Famous theaters

Theaters were first used to perform plays over 5,000 years ago. Today's famous theaters stage not only plays, but also operas, ballets, mime and music. Some of the best known are the Bolshoi in Moscow, Sydney Opera House, the Globe in London, New York's Radio City Hall, and the National Noh Theater in Tokyo.

Bolshoi Theater, Moscow, Russia

The Bolshoi is one of the best-known theaters in Europe, famous for its ballet and opera. More than a million people see shows here every year. The Bolshoi dates back to 1776, when Empress Catherine the Great granted Prince Pyotr Urusov the right to run "all the theatrical performances in Moscow." The first two theaters were destroyed by fires, and the present building dates from 1856.

⬥ There is hardly any scenery and very few props in a Japanese Noh theater.

National Noh Theater, Tokyo, Japan

The actors in traditional Japanese Noh theaters are all men. They perform on a small square stage which projects into the auditorium, forming a kind of theater-in-the-round. There is no curtain—the actors enter and exit the stage over a bridge connected to the backstage area. There is hardly any scenery, and very few props. The National Noh Theater in Tokyo opened in 1983, with seats for almost 600 people. Parts of the building are made from 2,000-year-old Japanese cypress trees.

◀ The Bolshoi Theater in Moscow. In the nineteenth century, many European theaters were built in the classical style of architecture. Their columns, roofs and decoration were based on ancient Greek buildings.

Opera House, Sydney, Australia

The Sydney Opera House is one of the busiest performing arts centers in the world, with over 2,000 performances a year. Beneath its concrete shells are five halls that stage symphony concerts, chamber music, operas, plays and exhibitions. The Opera House also has three restaurants, six bars and 60 dressing rooms.

⬤ The Opera House in Sydney took 14 years to build and was opened in 1973. More than one million tiles cover the roof of the building.

Globe Theatre, London, UK

The original Globe Theatre opened on the south bank of the River Thames in 1599. It survived until 1642, when the building was demolished. An accurate replica was opened in 1997, built 183 metres from the original site. Every summer it stages plays by Shakespeare and his contemporaries, on the type of open-air stage they were written for. The audience stands in wooden bays around the circular stage. Each bay is three stories high and has a roof thatched with reeds.

⬤ Audiences at the Globe Theatre can see performances similar to those of the 1600s. Spectators stand around the open-air stage to watch the show.

Radio City Music Hall, New York, USA

Radio City is one of the largest indoor theaters in the world, with seats for 6,000 people. Since it opened in 1932, more than 300 million people have enjoyed shows there. Four hydraulic lifts raise and lower the floor of the huge stage. During Christmas shows, the lifts allow the orchestra to disappear under the front of the stage, eventually reappearing high up at the back.

◗ The massive stage of New York's Radio City Music Hall makes the performers seem tiny.

Glossary

act One section of a play.

apron The narrow strip of the stage nearest the audience, in front of the curtain.

auditorium The part of the theater where the audience sits.

backdrop A large cloth decorated with a scene, also called a backcloth. It hangs at the back of the stage, and is hoisted into the flies when not in use.

baton A thin stick used by the conductor of an orchestra to beat time to music.

beamlight A lamp that shines a very strong, fixed beam of light. Beamlights are often used to show sunlight on stage.

box A private balcony for a small group of people in the auditorium.

box office The counter inside the foyer where tickets are sold.

cast The actors who take part in a show.

cue sheet A list showing when actors enter and exit the stage, and when light and sound effects are needed during a show.

curtain up The start of a show.

cyclorama A curved, plain cloth at the back of the stage which represents the sky. It is also called a skycloth.

director The person who is responsible for the overall look of a show. The director also gives the actors guidance on how to play their parts.

downstage The part of the stage nearest the audience.

dress circle The seats on the first floor of the auditorium.

dress rehearsal A rehearsal which is as close to a real performance as possible. The show is performed straight through without stopping, with light and sound effects, and scene changes. The actors wear full costume and make-up.

dresser An assistant who helps an actor backstage.

dressing A prop that decorates a set, but which is not used by an actor, such as a pot plant.

flat A screen painted with a scene, made from canvas or felt stretched over a wooden frame.

flies The high space above the stage where lights, scenery and backdrops are kept. The flies are also known as the fly tower.

floodlight A lamp that floods the stage with a wide beam of light.

fly bar A metal bar held in the flies by ropes. Ropes, backdrops, lanterns and other equipment are attached to them.

forestage A movable stage which can be placed over the pit when it is not in use.

furnishing A prop that decorates a set and is used by an actor, such as an armchair.

gallery Seats on the top floor of the auditorium, also known as the gods.

gauze A finely woven fabric used in special effects. It can appear transparent (see-through) or opaque (not see-through) depending on the type of light shone on to it.

gel A sheet of colored plastic which is attached to the front of a lamp to change the color of the light.

gobo A thin sheet of metal with a pattern cut out of it. It is attached to a spotlight, which then projects a shaped beam of light on to the stage.

gods Another name for the gallery.

greasepaint A type of greasy make-up used by actors.

green room A quiet room, used by the cast before and after a performance. Some green rooms also have a café.

hand prop A small prop handled by an actor, such as an umbrella.

Noh Traditional Japanese drama.

pit A sunken area between the stalls and the stage where the orchestra sits.

playhouse A type of circular theater building dating from the 1500s. Most of the audience stood up to watch a show.

playwright A person who writes plays.

prompt desk A desk tucked inside a wing. The stage manager runs the show from here.

props Furniture and other objects used by the cast during a performance. The word props is short for properties.

proscenium arch A decorative arch that frames the acting area.

pyrotechnics A type of special effect that uses explosives to make bangs, flashes and smoke.

rake The slope of some theater stages.

read-through An early rehearsal at which the script is read from start to finish.

rehearsal A practice session for the cast and technicians.

run A series of performances of the same show.

run-through A reading of the play at a rehearsal. The actors go through the whole play without stopping. They do not usually wear costumes or make-up.

safety curtain A fireproof shutter made from steel. It is also called the iron curtain or the fire curtain.

scenery All the painted backdrops and flats that show where a play is set.

script The written words, or text, of a play.

set All the scenery, furniture and props used in a scene.

sightline An imaginary line from the eye of a theater spectator to the edge of the stage. It is used to make sure that the audience has a clear view of the acting area.

spotlight A lamp that shines a strong beam of light on to a small area of the stage.

stage The area on which actors, singers and dancers perform.

stage manager The person who makes sure a performance runs smoothly.

stagehand Someone who moves props and pieces of scenery into position.

stagehouse The part of the theater building that contains the stage.

stalls The seats on the ground floor of the auditorium.

superstition An unusual or eccentric belief that has no evidence to support it.

theater-in-the-round A type of theater building in which the audience surrounds the stage area.

thespian Another name for an actor. Thespis, an ancient Greek poet, was the winner of the first-ever drama competition, in 534 BC.

tragedy A serious play, usually ending with the death of most of the main characters.

trap A section of the stage floor that opens into the area below the stage. It is also called a trap door or a stage trap.

understudy An actor who learns a part being played by another actor. The understudy can take over the role in an emergency.

upstage The back of the stage, furthest from the audience.

usher Someone who shows the audience to their seats.

wings The backstage area, on either side of the stage.

Index

First published in the United States in 2000 by Peter Bedrick Books
A division of NTC/Contemporary Publishing Group
4255 West Touhy Avenue, Lincolnwood (Chicago), Illinois, 60712-1975, USA

Copyright © Belitha Press Limited 2000
Text copyright © John Malam 2000

Theater cutaway illustrations: David Cuzik
Other illustrations: William Donohoe
Series editor: Mary-Jane Wilkins
Editor: Russell Mclean
Series designer: Guy Callaby
Designer: Jamie Asher
Picture researcher: Diana Morris
Consultants: Ayyub Malik and William James
Series concept: Christine Hatt

If you would like to comment on this book, e-mail the author at johnmalam@aol.com

The author and publishers wish to thank the Palace Theatre (part of the Apollo Leisure Group), Manchester, England for helping with this book.

ISBN 0-87226-588-9

Printed in China

Library of Congress Cataloging-in-Publication Data is available from the United States Library of Congress.

Picture acknowledgments:
Fotostock BV/Powerstock: 28b. A.Gin/Powerstock: 29t. Pete Jones/Performing Arts Library: 29bl. Paolo Koch/Robert Harding P.L: 28t. E.Young/ Art Directors & Trip P.L.: 29br.

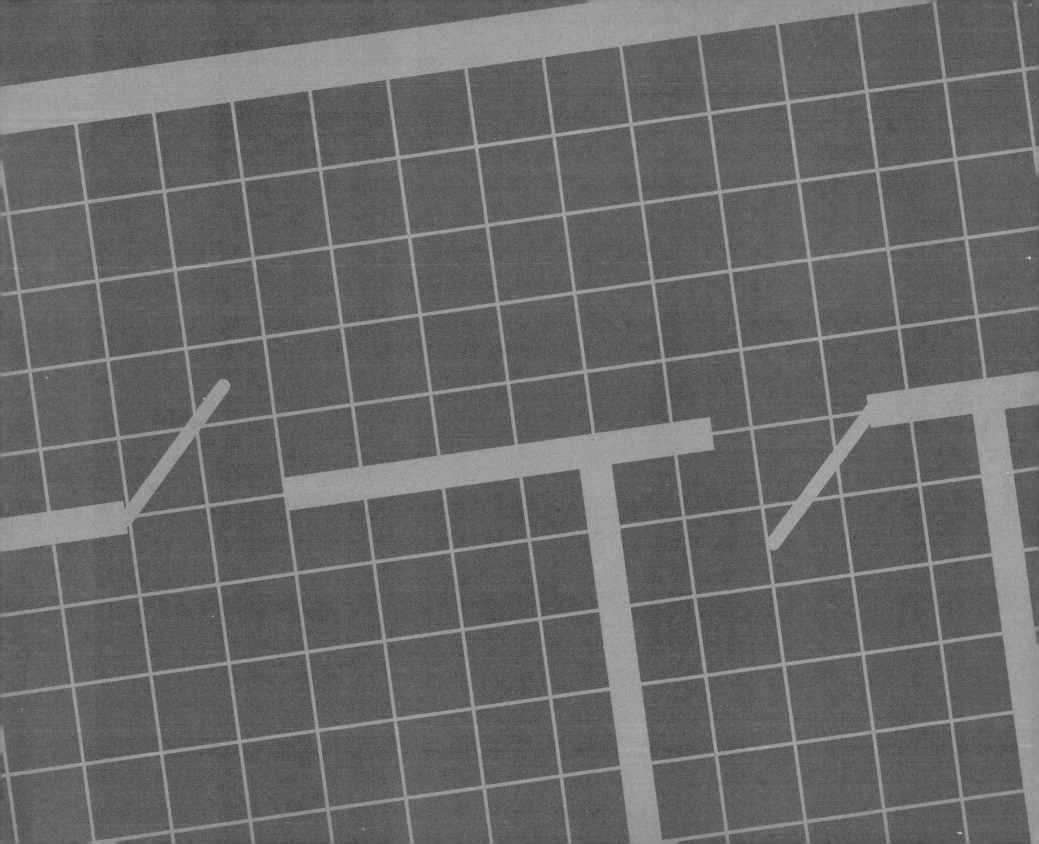